Thank you to my art teacher, Hannah Miller, for helping me with the illustrations. When the Corona pandemic hit, she even helped me over FaceTime.

I hope you enjoy this story!

Published by Argyle Fox Publishing | argylefoxpublishing.com
ISBN 978-1-953259-04-2 (Paperback)

Once there was an acorn that did
not want to leave her mom tree.

She loved having

funny conversations

with her brother

and sister acorns.

Knock knock!

Who's there?

Boo!

Boo who?

Don't cry!

But then a truck **hit** the tree

and the little
acorn

fell
and landed

in the back of the truck.

The truck ***drove away***

with the little acorn in it.

The truck hit a bump, and

the little acorn fell out of

the truck and landed in a

patch of grass.

At that, the acorn was *terrified*, lost,

and a l o n g way from home.

She was so sad,

so she decided to go to sleep.

When she woke up, she
realized she was a little
sprout. Now she could
see over the grass.

And every day she grew
a little bit more until
she stopped growing.

Now she could see all the way to

her old home.

She was so *happy* to see her mom.

Then she realized she had little

acorns of her own.

Sup
Hi
Hi

THE END

Leia Armbrust lives with her parents and three siblings in South Carolina.

She loves writing, sports, creating lovely art, going to the beach, and anything to do with being in the water.

Made in the USA
Columbia, SC
26 September 2020